CCSS Genre Exposi...

Essential Quest.....

What benefits come from people working as a group?

The Power of a Team

BY MARIA GILL

Introduction

Have you noticed that it's easier to solve problems when you work with other people? Sometimes they can look at the problem in a new way. Other times, you have done all you can and you need someone else to finish. Science is just the same.

Scientists from all over the world work in teams to answer questions. Some teams look for a cure for a disease. Others try to discover more about space.

Scientists often work together.

People with different skills can **collaborate**, or work together. This teamwork can lead to great **results**. They can find answers a lot faster by sharing their ideas.

A TEAM EFFORT

Howard Florey was an Australian scientist. He was one of the first people to get a team of scientists to work together. He was looking for better ways to treat infections. However, the problem was too big to solve on his own.

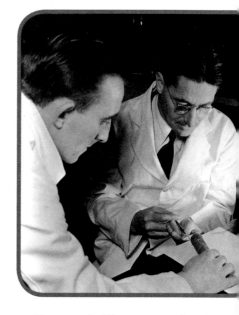

The team wanted to learn more about penicillin. Each scientist researched the uses of penicillin in their area. Then they shared their discoveries. Their work helped to find a cure for many common illnesses.

Howard Florey and his team saved thousands of lives.

Scientists at **NASA** also work in teams. One team planned, built, and launched two robots. It took three years. The robots were built to **rove**, or travel, across Mars. They could scan rocks and soil. Then the robots would send the data back to Earth.

The team had to find a place on Mars to land the robots safely. They picked two sites that looked like they used to have water. The robots lifted off in 2003.

The robots' names were *Spirit* and *Opportunity*. This is *Opportunity*.

It took about seven months to reach Mars. *Spirit* landed safely, but then there was a problem. An **air bag** was blocking the ramp out of the **lander**. The team knew what to do. The driver in the control room turned *Spirit* around and drove the robot down a side ramp instead.

Opportunity landed safely three weeks later. The team could relax. Their hard work had paid off.

The team gets the news that *Spirit* has arrived safely.

Spirit explored Mars for the next few months. Then its back wheel burst. The team found ways to keep the rover going. Sometimes they drove it in reverse.

Then *Spirit* got stuck in the soil. The team set up a sand trap on Earth to **mimic** *Spirit's* problem. They studied a model of the stuck rover and thought about how to free it. They tried out their ideas on the model.

Freeing *Spirit* led to a discovery. When *Spirit's* wheel dug into the soil, it uncovered a **substance**, or material, called silica. The silica showed scientists that there had been water on Mars in the past.

Team members use a model rover. This helps them try out different ways to get *Spirit* unstuck on Mars.

Opportunity spent two years roving around Mars before it reached a large crater. Then it spent over a year exploring the **crater**. The data *Opportunity* sent back will help geologists learn about the history of Mars.

Opportunity sent back images of craters on the surface of Mars.

Spirit stopped sending **signals**, or messages, to Earth in 2010. *Opportunity* is still roving across Mars.

A NASA EXPERIENCE

Thirteen teams of high school students and teachers worked with NASA scientists. They helped during launches and landings of the rovers. The students woke up at 4:00 A.M. for team meetings. They had jobs to do and attended press conferences. The students saw how everyone on the team worked together.

The next mission sent a new kind of robot to Mars. The Mars Science Laboratory, also called *Curiosity,* is the size of a car.

Curiosity landed on Mars on August 6, 2012. It has tools for collecting and **analyzing**, or studying, rock and soil samples. It has found evidence that water once flowed on the surface of Mars.

STOP AND CHECK

What did scientists do when *Spirit* got stuck?

This image shows *Curiosity* on Mars. It is using a laser to vaporize rocks. The rock dust can then be analyzed by special tools.

In 1964, two scientists at Bell Labs found something important by accident.

Arno Penzias and Robert Wilson were using a huge antenna to study radio waves in space. They kept hearing an annoying sound. It was like static. They pointed the antenna in other directions, but the noise did not go away. They thought bird droppings might be the problem. But when they cleaned the antenna, the hissing sound was still there.

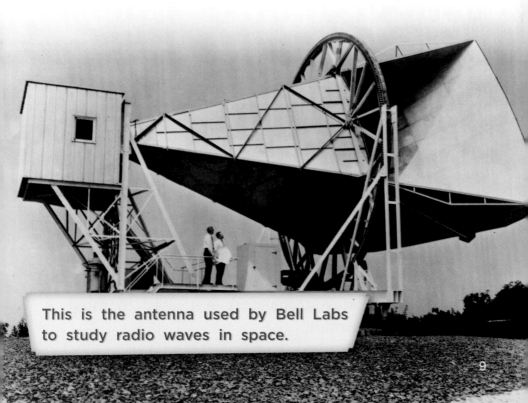

This is the antenna used by Bell Labs to study radio waves in space.

Scientists at Princeton University were studying the **big bang theory**. This theory says the universe was formed in a huge explosion. The explosion might have left behind low-level **radiation**. The scientists at Princeton and Bell Labs talked. They realized the antenna was picking up this low-level radiation.

That hissing sound is now called cosmic microwave background radiation. The scientists at Bell Labs won the **Nobel Prize** for their discovery.

A SMALL INVENTION WITH A BIG IMPACT

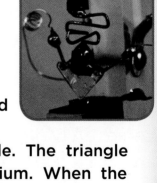

In the 1940s, a scientist wanted to make telephone signals stronger. He got a team of scientists to help him. For two years, they failed. Then they tried a new idea. They wrapped gold foil around a small plastic triangle. The triangle touched a mineral called germanium. When the scientists sent a signal through the triangle, the signal came out stronger. The team had succeeded!

Their work helped them build a device called a transistor. Today, transistors are used in most electronic equipment.

Scientists at Bell Labs are still working hard. They are looking for ways to help people communicate better. One team thinks that the human body might have the answer.

A network is equipment that is linked together. You use a communication network to surf the Internet or make a phone call. When you dial a friend's number, the network picks up a signal. Then the network carries the signal to your friend's phone.

Humans love to share information.

That's similar to how the nerves in your skin work. If you are cold, your nerves send a message to your brain. The message is picked up by the nervous system. Then it is carried to your brain.

Our nerves send lots of signals to our brains. They don't need our help. They just do it. However, communication networks do need our help. If they get too many signals, they can stop working, or jam.

Bell Labs wants to invent **flexible** networks. These would handle lots of signals **automatically**, without anyone telling them what to do, just like our bodies. Team members around the world are working on this idea.

STOP AND CHECK

What did the Bell Labs scientists discover by accident?

People want to stay connected everywhere they go.

12

Sometimes people work together for personal reasons. That's the case with The Miami Project.

Marc and Nick Buoniconti raise money for spinal research.

Marc Buoniconti was hurt playing football when he was 19. His spine was crushed, and he was paralyzed. Marc's father, Nick, wanted his son to walk again. Nick helped start The Miami Project. The Project does research to find a cure for paralysis. Marc is now president of The Miami Project.

SPINAL CORD INJURIES

Signals from our nerves travel through the body. They go up the spinal cord to the brain. The brain also sends signals down the spinal cord to the body. The spinal cord is a long bundle of nerves. It is protected by small bones called vertebrae. Marc's spinal cord was so badly damaged that his brain could not communicate with his body.

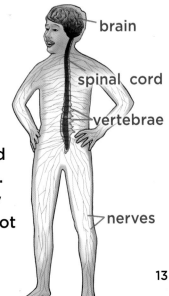

brain

spinal cord

vertebrae

nerves

Scientists around the world work on The Miami Project. Some are studying ways to prevent spinal cord damage. Another team is finding ways to help patients recover.

The team thinks that cooling the body down right after a spinal cord **injury** helps prevent more damage. They tested this on patients. Doctors lowered their body temperatures. Then the doctors slowly warmed the patients up again.

After a year, these patients could move more than the usual patients with spinal cord injuries. The team plans an even bigger **trial** with hundreds of patients.

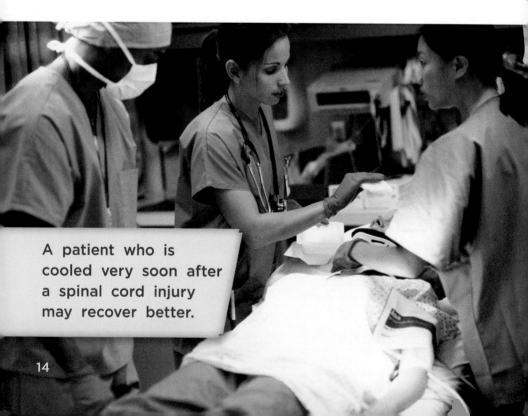

A patient who is cooled very soon after a spinal cord injury may recover better.

Other Miami Project scientists are working on ways to repair spinal tissue. They think that injecting special cells into a damaged area might help. These cells are called Schwann cells. They have an important **function**. Schwann cells make a substance called myelin. Myelin is important because it helps the nervous system communicate.

Researchers tested their idea on paralyzed rats. The rats got back 70 percent of their ability to walk. Now scientists are planning a trial with human patients.

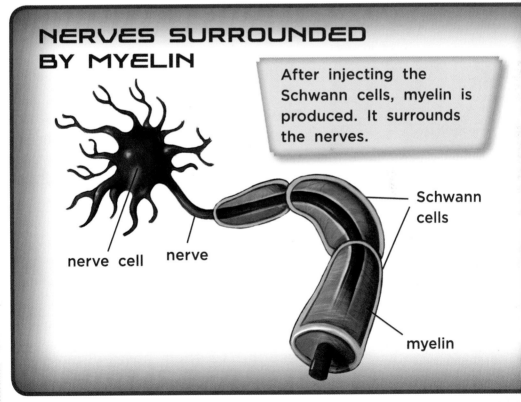

NERVES SURROUNDED BY MYELIN

After injecting the Schwann cells, myelin is produced. It surrounds the nerves.

Schwann cells

nerve cell   nerve

myelin

The Miami Project's scientists are also finding out how exercise helps people recover. Others are working on **techniques** to reduce patients' pain.

Scientists have learned that combining treatments can help people recover. Teams in different research areas are working together. They all have the same goal. They are **dedicated** to helping people with spinal injuries walk again.

STOP AND CHECK

What did The Miami Project scientists discover?

Dr. James McClurkin wants robots to work together.

ROBOT TEAMS

What if we sent a team of 200 robots to Mars, not just two? How much more could we learn? Dr. James McClurkin wants to find out. He works on multi-robot swarms. These are groups of robots that work together.

The robots communicate and work as a team. Dr. McClurkin was inspired by honeybees. Honeybees communicate and respond to their environment as a group.

Conclusion

Scientists and experts can get better results when they work together.

The noise that scientists at Bell Labs heard was a missing piece in the big bang puzzle. It took hundreds of people to put the rovers on Mars.

Scientists can make faster **progress** by sharing ideas. They can solve problems more quickly when they work together. One day they may be able to bring rocks back from Mars. Or they may help paralyzed people to walk again.

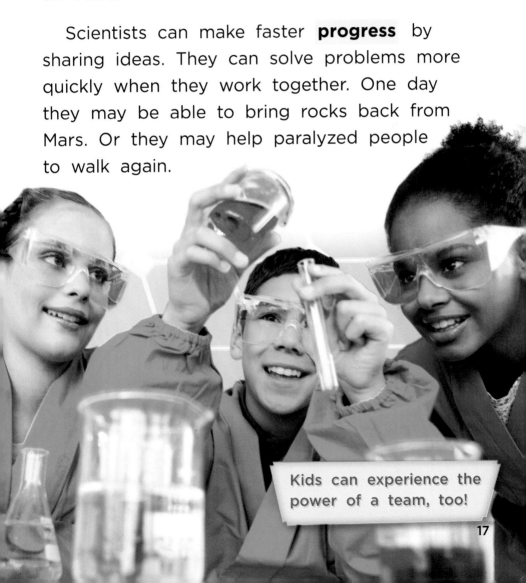

Kids can experience the power of a team, too!

Summarize

Summarize the main ideas from *The Power of a Team*. Use important details from the text. Your graphic organizer may help you.

Main Idea
Detail
Detail
Detail

Text Evidence

1. What is the main idea of Chapter 1? Give key details to support your answer. **MAIN IDEA AND KEY DETAILS**

2. Find the word *recover* on page 14. Use clues in the paragraph to help you figure out what the word means. **VOCABULARY**

3. Write about the main idea on page 14. Use key details from the text in your answer. **WRITE ABOUT READING**

Compare Texts

Read about how a team developed a special steering wheel.

HANDS ON THE WHEEL

A team of students from New Hampshire entered a science contest. They had to find a way to help people pay attention while they were driving.

The student scientists worked in stages. First, they studied the things that keep drivers from paying attention, such as texting. They learned that New Hampshire had just banned texting while driving.

Texting while driving is dangerous. The students wanted to stop this kind of unsafe driving.

Then the team observed drivers. They saw that drivers who were texting held the wheel a certain way.

The team shared ideas. They decided to make a device for steering wheels. The device beeps when drivers hold the steering wheel in an unsafe way. They worked with the Massachusetts Institute of Technology. They used an **artificial** driving machine to help them improve their model.

The team built eight different models. One model was too loud. The beep actually distracted drivers! The team fixed it. They also made the device wireless. This model was safer to use because it had no wires to catch the drivers' fingers in.

HOW IT WORKS

The invention is a steering-wheel cover. There are sensors around the edges of the cover. They tell where the driver's hands are on the wheel. If the driver's hands are in an unsafe place on the wheel, the device beeps and lights flash. This makes the driver refocus.

The team won the challenge. They call their solution the SMARTwheel™. Now they have applied for a **patent**. This will keep other people from copying their invention.

The team doesn't want any **obstacles** to stop the invention from being sold. They believe it will reduce the number of car crashes.

A team member looks at a SMARTwheel™ model.

Make Connections

What other people did the team work with to help them design their steering wheel? ESSENTIAL QUESTION

The scientists in *The Power of a Team* and the students in *Hands on the Wheel* worked in groups. How did teamwork help their projects succeed? TEXT TO TEXT

Glossary

air bag *(ayr bag)* a giant bag that inflates to cushion a lander's landing on Mars *(page 5)*

big bang theory *(big bayng THEER-ee)* the theory that the universe was formed from a huge explosion *(page 10)*

crater *(KRAY-tuhr)* a dish-shaped depression caused by a volcanic eruption or an object such as a meteorite slamming into the ground *(page 7)*

lander *(LAN-duhr)* a protective spacecraft carrying the rover robot *(page 5)*

NASA *(NA-suh)* National Aeronautics and Space Administration, the United States' space exploration agency *(page 4)*

Nobel Prize *(noh-BEL prighz)* an international award given for major advances in knowledge *(page 10)*

patent *(PAT-uhnt)* a way of legally protecting an invention so someone else can't copy it *(page 21)*

radiation *(ray-dee-AY-shuhn)* waves of energy sent out by sources of heat or light, including the sun *(page 10)*

trial *(trighl)* an experiment to test whether a theory is correct *(page 14)*

Index

Focus on Science

Purpose To show how a team can create a plan for a product using inquiry and technology

Procedure

Step 1 Work with a partner or in a small group. Think about a problem you would like to solve using technology.

Step 2 Think of a product you could make to solve this problem. Talk about what the product will do. Why is it needed?

Step 3 Draw your product.

Step 4 Now talk about who you will need on your team. What kinds of people or skills will you need to produce your product?

Conclusion To do something well, it is almost always better to work as a group. You get the knowledge and skills of each member of the team. What are some of the other benefits of teamwork?